D0852359

DE?

A FAMILY TREASURY OF

Bible Stories

One for Each Week of the Year

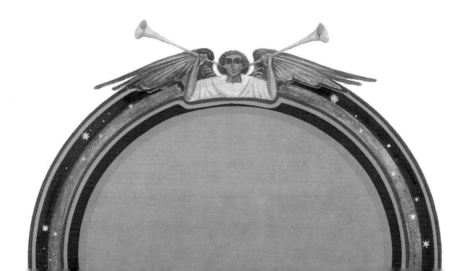

The Lord is my shepherd, I shall not want;
he makes me lie down in green pastures.
He leads me beside still waters; he restores my soul.
He leads me in paths of righteousness for his name's sake.
Even though I walk through the valley
of the shadow of death,
I fear no evil; for thou art with me;
thy rod and thy staff, they comfort me.
Thou preparest a table before me in the presence of my enemies;
thou anointest my head with oil, my cup overflows.
Surely goodness and mercy shall follow me all the days of my life;
and I shall dwell in the house of the Lord forever.

Psalm 23

A FAMILY TREASURY OF
Bible Stories

One for Each Week of the Year

As told by Roberto Brunelli

Illustrations by Mikhail Fiodorov

Translated from the Italian by Lawrence Jenkens

Harry N. Abrams, Inc., Publishers

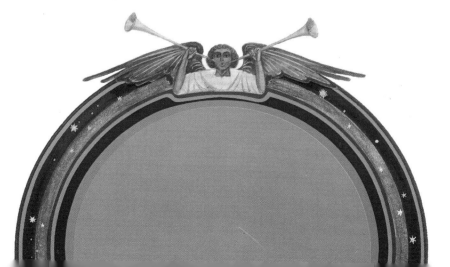

Contents

OLD TESTAMENT

NEW TESTAMENT

What the Bible Is

The Lord sent a letter to all people. It is a beautiful piece of writing, full of interesting and important things. It is so big that a book was made of it; that book is the Bible.

Our word *Bible,* which comes from the Greek language, means "books." Indeed, the Bible is made up of seventy-three different books,* some written by and for the Jews who lived before Christ and some by and for the Christian community of the first century after Christ.

The Bible is unlike any other book. It was written by different people over the course of many centuries, although these people were all guided by God so that they would tell what He wanted to say to all of us. In this way the Bible really is like a letter written by the Lord.

The seventy-three books of the Bible are divided into the Old Testament and the New Testament. A testament is a pact or an alliance, and it refers to the alliance which God, in ancient times, made with the people of Israel and to a new alliance which God made with all people through Jesus Christ.

The Old Testament consists of forty-six books which, with a few exceptions, make up that part of the Bible used by the Jews. The first five books – Genesis, Exodus, Leviticus, Numbers, and Deuteronomy – are called the Pentateuch, which, in fact, means "five books." The Jews call this the Torah, which means the Law. They were written a long time ago, between the thirteenth and the sixth centuries before Christ. The other books of the Old Testament, written between the eleventh and the second centuries before Christ, all have different narrators who tell the history of the Jews. They also contain the prophecies of the prophets and the lessons and wisdom that explain these teachings.

The New Testament has twenty-seven books which were written in the second half of the first century after Christ. The first four are the Gospels; they tell the life of Christ and his teachings, each according to the particular point of view of the evangelist who wrote it. Matthew, who was also one of Christ's disciples, wrote to convince the Jews that Jesus is the Messiah whose coming was foretold by the Old Testament prophets. Mark, a disciple of St. Peter, wanted to show the non-Christians that Jesus is the Son of God. Luke, who was a non-Christian and a doctor before becoming a follower of St. Paul, seeks to show that Jesus is the Savior of all humankind. John, also an apostle of Christ, recounts many stories that the other evangelists did not tell.

The Acts of the Apostles follow the Gospels. Here Luke the Evangelist tells about the lives of the first Christians and records the letters of the apostles, especially Paul's, which were addressed to many Christian communities and to his helpers and friends. The New Testament ends with the Book of Revelation, which is also called the Apocalypse, a book of prophesy written by John the Evangelist.

Let us read together the selection of Bible stories gathered in this book. These are not meant to replace the Bible itself; rather, through the stories, the explanations, and the illustrations that follow we will begin to understand something of this marvelous and rich letter that the Lord sent to all people of all times. This letter is meant to console us in our sorrows, to guide our way through life, to nourish our hopes, to answer our most difficult questions, and to bring us to true and complete happiness, a happiness that we can one day have with God in heaven.

*In different versions of the Bible, the number of books varies. The Douay version includes forty-six Old Testament books and twenty-seven New Testament ones. The biblical references that appear in this book are cited from that version. The King James Version, the Revised Standard Version, and other modern versions accept only sixty-six books as canonical.

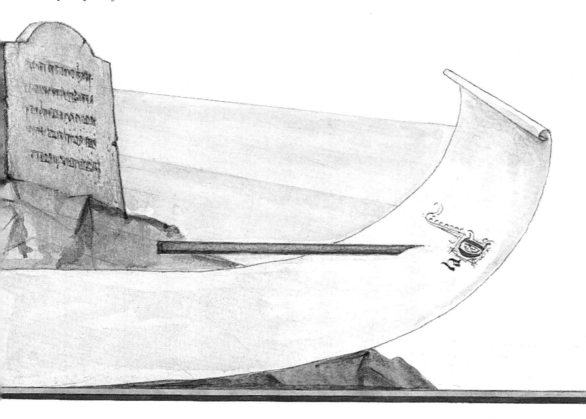

OLD TESTAMENT

Hear, O Israel: The Lord our God is one Lord;
and you shall love the Lord your God with all your heart,
and with all your soul, and with all your might.
And these words which I command you this day
shall be upon your heart; and you shall teach them diligently
to your children, and shall talk of them when you sit
in your house, and when you walk by the way,
and when you lie down, and when you rise.

Deuteronomy 6:4–7

The Creation

*I*n the beginning, before there was the world, there was God. He has always existed.

Then God decided to create the universe. With His mighty voice He called into being one thing after another that had not been there before.

He said, "Let there be light," and there was light. He separated it from darkness and called it day. The darkness he called night.

The next day God made the sky and spread it like a giant vault over the earth.

On the third day He separated the dry land from the waters of the sea, and on that land He made grass, flowers, and fruit trees grow.

On the fourth day God made two lights in the sky so that people could measure the years, the months, and the days. The greater light, the sun, He gave to daytime and the smaller, the moon, to the night. He also made the stars.

The world God created was very beautiful, but it was not

enough. On the fifth day God put fish in the seas and made all sorts of birds to fly in the sky.

On the sixth day God created all the animals, from the smallest to the very largest, that would live on the earth. But this was still not enough. God said, "Let us make man in our own image and likeness. He will rule over the fish in the sea, over the birds in the sky, and the animals on the earth." God created man and wished him to be made in His image and likeness.

Satisfied with His work, God rested on the seventh day, and this is how the first week of the world unfolded. Since then, in order to do as God did, people have counted the days in weeks. The first six days are for work, but the seventh is for rest and to give us the leisure to think with gratitude of God, the Lord and Creator, who gave to all humankind dominion over the world which He created.

Adam and Eve

Genesis 2–3

God did not want man to be alone, and so He made a woman to be man's wife. He called the man Adam and the woman Eve and set them both in a marvelous garden called Eden, rich with all types of fruit that were good to eat. The Lord told them to take all the fruit that they wanted except that of one particular tree. "That is the tree of knowledge of good and evil," He said. "You must not eat its fruit, because if you do you will die."

This is what the Lord said.

With this one, small forbidden thing, God wanted to test Adam and Eve to see if they loved Him and therefore trusted Him. But instead they listened to another, a clever demon who envied them their happiness and wished to destroy it. The demon took the form of a serpent and tempted Eve, saying, "It isn't true that you would die. God forbade you to eat these fruits to stop you from knowing all about good and evil. Otherwise you would become just like Him!"

The woman gave in. She picked a fruit from the tree of knowledge, took a bite, and gave the fruit to Adam, who also ate a piece. Immediately both understood that they had done wrong not to trust in the Lord; they felt ashamed and were terribly unhappy.

The consequences were severe. They had to leave the marvelous garden of Eden. In order to eat, they had to work the earth, and their life became full of weariness, worries, and pain. They had disobeyed and thus had ruined the plans made by God, who had wanted them to be happy.

Cain and Abel

From that day on, sin, which is disobedience of God, multiplied. We encounter it again very soon in the story of Cain and Abel, the two sons of Adam and Eve.

Cain became a farmer and Abel a shepherd. One day the two made an offering to God of the best fruits of their labor. God, who can read what is in our hearts, accepted Abel's offering but not Cain's. Cain became jealous of his brother, and his anger grew and grew until one day he invited Abel to his fields and killed him.

God, who sees everything, asked him, "Where is your brother?" and Cain, adding lies to his crime, retorted, "How should I know? Am I my brother's keeper? Must I always know where he is?"

The Lord then said, "Because you have killed your brother, you must go away. You will wander like a nomad for the rest of your life."

Cain was afraid that someone would kill him, but God did not want anyone to die, even one who had committed such grave sins. For this reason He put a sign on Cain, a warning that none should do him harm.

15

The Great Flood

Much time passed after these events. The number of people on earth grew, as did their sins. They became mean and selfish and disobedient to the Lord. The one exception was a man called Noah and his family. Because he was good, God ordered Noah to build an ark – a big boat – for himself, his wife, his sons, and their wives, and a pair of each species of animal.

When everything was ready, God made it rain over the whole earth for forty days and forty nights without stopping. The water covered everything except the ark, which floated on the water and kept all those inside it safe. That enormous flood – the Great Flood – spared only those inside the ark.

When the rains ended, the waters receded, and the ark came to rest on a mountain called Ararat. Noah opened a window and let a dove fly out. The dove, however, found nowhere to land and flew back to the ark. Seven days later, Noah again released the dove, which came back this time with a twig of an olive tree in its beak. Noah understood then that the water was gone. After waiting another seven days, the dove was released once again, and this time it did not come back.

Noah then opened the door,

Genesis 6—9

and the animals left the ark to repopulate the earth.

Noah and his family also left the ark and gave thanks to the Lord for having saved them from the flood. God then promised them, "There will never be another flood. As a sign of this promise, I am putting a rainbow in the sky."

The Tower of Babel

Much time went by after the Great Flood. The descendants of Noah multiplied and became a great people who lived on a fertile plain. They used their intelligence to make the land produce all the food they needed, and they were skilled in their labors, which included weaving cloth, making tools, raising livestock, and building houses.

But over time these people had forgotten what God had done for them and had even forgotten that God saved them from the flood. They had again begun committing sins, and one sin in particular. The descendants of Noah believed that they were intelligent and capable enough to decide by themselves, as if they were God, what was good or bad and right or wrong. This sin is called pride.

Their pride led them one day to make a big decision. "Let us make enough bricks," they said, "to build an entire city, and in that city we will construct a huge tower tall enough to touch the sky. Everyone will be able to see it from far away, and we will be united by what we have done. Furthermore, the tower will last for centuries, and those who see it after us will know what great builders we were."

As soon as that was said, everyone began to work hard, and quickly the tower began to rise from its foundations. It grew above the houses, to the tops of the palm trees, and then higher and higher, until it seemed to be lost among the clouds.

God, naturally, saw all this coming and going, and He realized that human beings had now excluded Him from their lives. He loved them, though, and could not allow the situation to continue because He knew nothing good would come of it for them.

So He intervened. Until that time everyone had spoken the

Genesis 11

same language, but from that moment on they spoke different languages. In this way they could no longer understand one another, and thus they could not work together. For this reason their city was called Babel, a name which means confusion.

The construction of the tower stopped. The people separated themselves according to the language they spoke, and in these groups they left the city and went in different directions to populate the earth.

The Calling of Abraham

Abraham was a shepherd who raised many sheep on the outskirts of a city in the east named Haran. Here he lived with his wife, Sarah, his relatives, and all the people who worked for him.

Like everyone else at that time, Abraham did not know the real God and worshiped the same divinity as the other people in that region. But when the real

God, the Lord, decided to make Himself known there, He chose to speak to Abraham. God reads people's hearts, and He knew He could trust Abraham.

One day the Lord called Abraham and said to him, "Leave your flock, your homeland, your father's house, and go to the land that I will tell you about. I will make you a father of children who will in turn have children,

until an entire people will have descended from you. I will make you famous and will shower you with gifts. Indeed, through you I will bless all the people of the earth."

God was certainly demanding! Abraham knew that, too, because God was asking him to leave behind everything he held dear, his city, his kinsmen and friends, and go to an unknown

place. Furthermore, Abraham and his wife were both old; they had no children, and they had by that time lost any hope of having them. How could he become the father of an entire people?

But God, in turning to Abraham, had shown that He trusted him, so Abraham decided to trust God. He took with him his wife and his nephew Lot, his dependents, his servants and his flock, and left his home.

From Haran he went toward the south. He crossed mountains and valleys and finally came to a land called Canaan. He traveled slowly through the region and, when he was close to the city of Shechem, he pitched his tents near an oak tree. Here the Lord spoke to him again and fulfilled the promise that He had made, saying, "I will give this region to your descendants."

This was the promised land. As the Lord had said, it became the land of the descendants of Abraham, the Jews, who changed its name and called it the Land of Israel.

Abraham and Isaac

Moving again within the promised land, Abraham pitched his tents under the oaks of Mamre, near Hebron. One day while he was seated outside his own tent, he looked up and saw three men standing in front of him. Following the customs of hospitality, he immediately had water brought to them so they could wash their feet. Then he went into his tent and told Sarah to prepare flatbread, and he chose a young calf and had it cooked. When all was ready, he offered the food to the three mysterious visitors.

When they had eaten, the three said, "We will return in a year, and at that time your wife, Sarah, will have had a child." Sarah, inside the tent, had been listening and at these words smiled unbelievingly, thinking, "I am too old to have a child!" But the three men were sent by the Lord and knew Sarah's thoughts. They said, "Why does your wife doubt us? Is there anything that is impossible for God?"

And indeed that is what happened. Before a year had passed, Abraham and Sarah had a baby, whom they named Isaac, which means "God has smiled." The baby grew up to be handsome and healthy. Abraham thanked God from the bottom of his heart. Isaac would have children, and his children other children, until they became a nation. God would give them this land in which they still lived as foreigners.

WEEK 8

The Sacrifice of Isaac

Genesis 22

One day God said to Abraham, "Take your son, your only son whom you love so much, and go up on the mountain that I will show you. There, I want you to sacrifice Isaac to me." Abraham did not understand. It was a terrible thing to ask him to kill his own son, his consolation, his only hope! Also, Abraham and Sarah were now even older. How would God's promise be realized?

Although he did not understand, Abraham decided again to put his trust in God. Early in the morning he saddled the donkey, chopped wood for the sacrifice, and, taking his son, Isaac, and two servants, started out for the place that God showed him. On the third day of travel he saw it. He left the servants with the donkey, loaded the wood on Isaac's shoulders, and climbed with him to the top of Mount Moriah. There he built an altar and spread the wood on top of it. He tied his son with rope, laid him across the wood, and picked up his knife. Just at that moment an angel of the Lord intervened. "Abraham, Abraham! Do not harm your boy! Now God knows that you fear Him and have not refused to give Him your only son." Then, raising his eyes, Abraham saw nearby a ram caught in a bush by its horns. He took it and sacrificed it in place of his son. God had put Abraham to the test, and Abraham had not failed Him.

Enemy Brothers: Jacob and Esau

Abraham died at a very old age. Isaac grew up and inherited the promises God had made to his father, Abraham. And he planned to pass them on in turn to his firstborn and favorite son, Esau. But Esau's twin brother, Jacob, wanted the rights of the oldest son for himself.

One day Esau returned home from hunting, tired and starving, and found that Jacob had prepared a dish of lentils.

"Give them to me, because I am hungry," Esau said to Jacob. And Jacob replied quickly, "Give me in exchange your rights as the firstborn." "I am dying of hunger. Of what use to me are my rights? Take them, by all means," his brother answered.

Thus Esau gave up his rights as the firstborn to Jacob, but it was still necessary to get the blessing of their father, Isaac.

This happened in the follow-

ing way. One day Isaac, who was very old and almost blind, called Esau to him and said, "You are a fine hunter. Go catch some game, make me a good dinner with it, and I will then give you my blessing before I die."

Isaac's wife, Rebecca, heard these words, and they displeased her. Of her two sons, she preferred Jacob and wanted him to inherit from his father. So, while Esau was away hunting, Rebecca

said to Jacob, "Bring me two young goats from the flock. I will cook them for your father, and he will give you his blessing."

"You know that my brother is very hairy," Jacob reminded her. "If my father touches me, he will know that I am not Esau." Rebecca replied, "Do as I tell you." Then she cooked the goats, made Jacob put on Esau's clothes, and then wound the skins of the goats around his neck and arms.

Once this was done, Jacob, pretending to be Esau, brought his father the food and asked for his blessing. Isaac made his son come close to him. He touched Jacob's hands and, mistaking him for his firstborn son, gave him his solemn blessing.

When he returned home and discovered the trick, Esau was very angry. It was too late, though, because once given, the blessing could not be taken back. Esau

swore that he would have his revenge and told Jacob, "When our father dies, I will kill you for what you have done to me."

Peace between Brothers; Jacob Becomes Israel

After these events, Rebecca thought it best to separate the two brothers, and she sent Jacob far away to stay with relatives who lived in Haran. There he remained for many years and became an able and prosperous livestock farmer. He married and had many children. Eventually, however, he decided to return home. Facing the risk of Esau's revenge but wanting to make peace with him, Jacob sent his brother many lavish gifts. These, however, were not necessary because by then Esau had forgotten the wrong done to him. The two brothers reconciled and, when it came time, they buried their father together.

Jacob was still his father's heir, and twice the Lord showed him His goodwill. One night, while Jacob was going to Haran, he lay down on the ground. As he slept he dreamed he saw a tall ladder stretching from the ground to the sky with God's angels climbing up and down it. The Lord Himself came to Jacob and said,

"I am the Lord God of Abraham and of Isaac. I will give you as many descendants as there are stars in the sky, and to them I will give the land that you are lying on now. I will protect you wherever you go and will make you return to this land someday."

Jacob awoke, full of fear, and cried out, "The Lord is in this place and I did not know it!" Then he made a pledge to remain faithful to God forever.

The second time God showed Jacob His goodwill was when he was returning from Haran. Jacob was traveling with his family and his flock but at a certain point found himself alone on the bank of the river Jabbok. It was nighttime. He was approached by a stranger, who engaged him in a wrestling match that lasted until dawn. When the stranger was about to leave, Jacob realized that he had been sent by God. So Jacob said, "I will not let you go until you have given me your blessing."

The stranger did bless him

Genesis 25–33

and added, "From now on I will no longer call you Jacob, but Israel, because you wrestled with me and you won."

In this way the people descended from Jacob, the Jews, are called the "children of Israel" and Israel is also called the land promised to them by God.

WEEK 10

Joseph the Dreamer

Jacob-Israel had twelve sons, but Joseph was his favorite. Joseph's brothers were jealous of him and became even more so when their father gave Joseph a beautiful new coat with long sleeves. Their envy turned into hatred when Joseph told his brothers about two dreams he had had. He said, "I dreamed we were in the field tying sheaves of wheat. My sheaf was in the middle and yours, in a circle around mine, bowed down to it. Then I dreamed that the sun, the moon, and eleven stars also paid homage to me."

In those days dreams were considered prophecies of events that would occur sooner or later. When Joseph said these things, his whole family began to worry. His father, speaking for all of them, said, "Are you saying

that all of us, including myself and your mother, will be subject to you?"

Sometime later Jacob sent Joseph to check on his brothers, who were pasturing their flocks far away from home. When they saw him coming, Joseph's brothers decided to kill him, throw his body into a well, and tell their father that a ferocious animal had torn him to pieces.

But the oldest brother, Ruben, thought of a plan to save him. He told his brothers to leave Joseph alive in the well, thinking that he would come back later and free him. The brothers agreed. They tore his shirt and threw him alive into the empty well. But just then a caravan of merchants passed by, and the brothers decided instead to sell Joseph as a slave to these mer-

chants. They pulled him from the well and sold him for twenty pieces of silver. Then they sprinkled goat's blood on the coat with the long sleeves. They took it to Jacob and used it to convince him that Joseph had been eaten by a wild beast.

Joseph, Viceroy of Egypt

The caravan went directly to Egypt. There Joseph was sold as a slave to a rich Egyptian, but very soon afterward he was falsely accused of a crime and put in prison. He found himself sharing a cell with two men, the chief baker and the chief butler of Pharaoh, the king of Egypt.

These men each had a dream and told it to Joseph.

"I dreamed that I had three bunches of grapes that I squeezed into a cup," said the butler.

"I dreamed of three baskets full of bread, but birds came and ate it all," said the baker.

And Joseph said, "The butler will be freed. The baker will be condemned to death." And that is what happened.

After two years Pharaoh also had a dream. None of the wise men of Egypt were able to explain it. The chief butler told the king that there was a Jew in his prison who could interpret dreams. Joseph was brought to the king, and he listened to the dream.

Pharaoh said, "I saw seven lean cows devour seven fat cows and seven withered ears of corn eat seven full ears of corn."

Joseph told him, "The two dreams mean the same thing. There will be seven years of plenty in Egypt, followed by seven years of famine. If you do not want your people to die, you must charge the wisest of your advisers with collecting enough

reserve food during the years of plenty to distribute during the famine."

Pharaoh said in return, "As God has shown you the meaning of the dreams, you must be the wisest of men. You must put the plan you have described into action."

Pharaoh gave Joseph his signet ring and placed a gold chain around his neck, and in this way, Joseph became viceroy of Egypt.

Joseph Forgives His Brothers; The People of Israel Go to Egypt

The things Joseph predicted came to pass in Egypt and in the way Joseph had said they would. During the years of plenty, he created enormous stocks of grain that, during the famine, he sold even to people from foreign lands.

The famine reached all the way to the place where Jacob lived with his other sons, who traveled to Egypt to buy grain. They did not know what had become of Joseph and did not recognize him when they appeared before him. But Joseph recognized them!

Hiding his surprise, Joseph managed not to give himself away. He had a plan. Speaking through a translator, he learned how his aged father, Jacob, was. Then he accused his brothers of

Joseph Forgives His Brothers; The People of Israel Go to Egypt

being spies sent by the enemies of Egypt to report on the situation there and had them thrown in prison. Later he let them return home but kept one of them, Simon, as a hostage. To free him they would have to bring the youngest brother, Benjamin, who had stayed at home with their father.

"Our father will die if we take away his youngest son. This is our punishment for what we did to Joseph!" They did not know that Joseph had understood them and was moved by what they said.

Only after the brothers had returned with Benjamin did Joseph tell them who he was. He said, "God decided to send me to Egypt because I could save you and your families here. Go and bring our father, your wives, children, and animals. From now on, you will live in safety in Egypt."

This came to pass. Jacob embraced Joseph, and from the twelve sons of Jacob are descended the twelve tribes of the people of Israel.

Moses Is Saved from the River; The Burning Bush

Many years passed after the Jews came to live in Egypt. As the people of Israel became more numerous and powerful, Pharaoh began to worry about them, and in order to reduce the growth in their numbers he placed them into slavery. He imposed on them cruel taskmasters, who forced them to break stones which were used for building new cities. He also ordered that all baby boys be put to death by throwing them into the river Nile as soon as they were born.

Moses Is Saved from the River; The Burning Bush

One, however, was saved. When they could no longer keep him hidden, his father and mother put him in a basket that would float and placed it in the water at the edge of the river. His sister watched what happened.

God decided that the daughter of Pharaoh, who had gone down to the river to bathe, would see the basket. When she picked it up she found the baby and took him to be her son. "I will call him Moses," she said. At that very moment the child's sister came up to her and asked her, "Would you like me to find a wet nurse among the women of Israel?"

The princess agreed, and the clever sister went to find her mother, who in this way was able to raise her son. When Moses was grown, the princess took

him back and had him educated as a prince at Pharaoh's court.

Moses knew he was an Israelite, and gradually he became unhappy about the hard conditions in which his people lived. One day, to defend one of his own people who was being mistreated, he killed an Egyptian.

To avoid being captured and put in prison, he fled. He crossed the desert and settled among the shepherds of the region called the Sinai.

Many years went by. Moses was tending his flocks in the hills when he saw a bush in flames. "How strange," he observed, "the bush burns but is not consumed!" He came closer to it, and from the bush a voice spoke out to him saying, "Moses, Moses! I am the Lord God of Abraham, Isaac, and Jacob. I have seen the suffering of My people

in Egypt and am sending you to free them. You will lead the Israelites out of Egypt, toward the land that I promised them."

Moses covered his eyes because he was afraid to look at God and then said, "Who am I, Lord, that Pharaoh would listen to me?" "I will be with you," the Lord reassured him. But Moses still said, "I am slow of speech and not eloquent."

The Lord then said, "You will teach your brother Aaron, and he will speak for you."

The Plagues of Egypt; The First Passover

Obeying God's command, Moses returned to Egypt. There he found his sister and met Aaron, his younger brother. He explained God's plan to his people and then, with Aaron, went to Pharaoh and said, "The God of Israel orders you to let His people go."

Pharaoh refused to let them go. Speaking through Aaron, Moses told him of the many punishments that the Lord would send to force him to free the people of Israel. And these punishments, the famous "plagues of Egypt," soon came. Water turned to blood, and frogs, flies, and gnats overran the countryside. Many livestock died; the fields were destroyed, first by hail and then by locusts. And then for three days all of Egypt was plunged into darkness.

All of this was in vain. With every disaster, Pharaoh promised

to let the people of Israel go and then, as soon as the plague ceased, he changed his mind. Then God told Moses of the last and worst punishment, the death of every firstborn Egyptian child, from Pharaoh's child to the child of the lowest servant. God also explained to Moses what the Israelites must do.

In the evening, every family of Israel took a lamb, cut its throat, and with its blood put a sign on the door of the house. Then they roasted the lamb over the fire and ate it together with bitter herbs. This was to remind them of the bitterness of slavery. They ate their meal standing up because they were just about to start on their voyage, and they also ate unleavened bread, which could be prepared quickly.

During the night, the angel of God passed through all the houses which were not marked with lamb's blood, that is to say, the Egyptian houses, and all the firstborn, including Pharaoh's, died. Terrified, Pharaoh called Moses and told him that he and his people must leave Egypt forever.

This meal was called Passover, which means passage. The angel had passed over the houses marked with blood, saving them from death. Since then Jews have celebrated Passover every year to remember this important event.

Freedom beyond the Sea; Miracles in the Desert

All the Israelites left Egypt, taking their household goods and their animals, and headed straight for the promised land. They had not been gone long when Pharaoh began to regret having allowed them to leave and decided to make them come back. Without slaves life would be hard for the Egyptians! He fitted out six hundred war chariots and set out to pursue the Israelites.

He caught up to them on the

shore of the sea that the Israelites would have to cross to be safe. How would they do it? With the water in front of them and the Egyptian army at their backs, the people of Israel said to Moses, "What have you done? It would have been better to remain slaves in Egypt than to die here in the desert!"

But Moses replied, "Do not be afraid; God is with us!" Then he raised his staff and spread his hand over the sea. The waters parted, and the Jews crossed to the opposite shore on dry land.

The Egyptians started to pursue them along the same path, but Moses spread out his hand again. The waters returned to where they were before, closing over the entire Egyptian army and drowning it.

The Lord continued to help His people in the desert, making sure that they found water and food.

One evening a great flock of quail flew down and landed near the encampment of the Israelites, who were able to capture many of them in flight.

Another time the Lord helped them by making water spring from the rocks. Yet again, early one morning, a layer of dew covered the ground. When it evaporated the Israelites found a fine, flaky substance spread over the desert. They tasted it and found that it was sweet and nourishing. It was manna. God fed His people with manna for the whole time they stayed in the desert.

Moses Receives the Ten Commandments; The Golden Calf

After several months of wandering in the region called the Sinai, the Israelites reached the foot of a tall mountain. Moses climbed to its summit, as the Lord had commanded him. There he stayed for forty days, :here the Lord gave him two : tablets on which were written ten rules – the Ten Commandments. The Lord said to Moses, "I will make a pact with My people. If they follow these rules, I will be their God. I will lead them and protect them."

Here are the Commandments:

1. I am the Lord your God. You shall have no other gods before me.
2. Do not take the name of the Lord in vain.
3. Remember to keep the sabbath day holy.
4. Honor your father and your mother.
5. Do not kill.
6. Do not commit adultery.
7. Do not steal.
8. Do not lie.
9. Do not long for another's wife.
10. Do not long for another's belongings.

Exodus 19–20; 32–34; 40

Moses stayed on the mountain for a long time talking with God. After a while the people of Israel, thinking that he would not come back and afraid that God had abandoned them in the desert, asked Aaron what to do. He gave them another god, first melting gold and then making it into the shape of a calf. Everyone began to worship the golden calf.

When Moses came down from the mountain, he saw what had happened and became angry. In his fury, he threw the tablets on the ground and broke them. He took the golden calf and destroyed it. Then he went back to the mountain to talk again to God. Out of His goodness God offered His forgiveness and gave Moses another two tablets, which the people solemnly promised to respect.

To preserve the memory of the pact between God and His people, Moses put both the tablets in a wooden box covered with gold. This box was called the Ark of the Covenant.

The Promised Land; The Conquest of Jericho

Before letting the people of Israel enter the promised land, Moses sent several of his men to explore it. The scouts returned, carrying a bunch of grapes so big that it could only be moved on a pole carried on the shoulders of two men. They also brought figs and pomegranates and said the land was so fertile and rich that it seemed to flow with milk and honey! But conquering it would not be easy because it was populated by strong warriors who lived in a city protected by high walls.

Joshua, Moses' successor as leader of the Israelites, was not daunted. When the time came, he led his people in their conquest of the promised land. He had faith in the Lord who had promised to give this land to His people.

And this is how the Lord helped His people to conquer the city of Jericho.

When the army of the Israelites arrived at Jericho, the citizens of that city, their king, and his soldiers, all shut themselves inside the town and barricaded the gates. They were convinced that they would be safe. Who, after all, could conquer such a strongly fortified city? But the Jews, following the instructions the Lord gave to Joshua, formed a procession. There were seven priests at the front, each with a trumpet; after them came the Ark of the Covenant, and Joshua followed with the soldiers. The procession moved around the walls of the city once a day for six days in a row. On the seventh day they walked around the city seven times in silence. Then, when the priests sounded their trumpets, everyone shouted loudly and the impossible happened: the walls of Jericho tumbled down!

The Israelites conquered other

Joshua 6

cities after Jericho and settled in the promised land, which has ever since been called the land of Israel. It was divided among the twelve tribes that made up the people of God. Each tribe occupied one region; all, however, came to pray in front of the Ark of the Covenant, which was the sign of the presence of God among His people.

WEEK 18

Samson and the Philistines

The Philistines were among the most dangerous enemies of the people of Israel. To fight them, the Lord chose from among His people Samson, a courageous young man endowed with extraordinary strength. He was so strong that once, when he was attacked by a lion, he killed it with his bare hands, not using any weapons. Another time he caught foxes and bound them together in pairs by their tails. He tied a lighted torch to them and let them loose in the Philistines' grain fields, which were ready to be harvested. The crops burned and their grapevines and olive groves were destroyed.

Samson was a real scourge, and his enemies wished to be rid of him. When he began visiting the house of Delilah, a Philistine woman whom he loved, the Philistines promised Delilah a large sum of money if she could discover the secret of his great strength. Delilah agreed and, after pressing him, succeeded in getting Samson to reveal the mystery.

"Before I was born," Samson confided, "my mother promised the Lord that I would dedicate myself completely to His service. As a sign of this I have never cut my hair. If I did my strength would vanish."

During the night, while Samson was sleeping, Delilah tied him up, cut his hair, and called in the Philistines. Samson, now deprived of his great strength, was put in prison, blinded, and forced to turn a millstone like a slave. The terrible enemy was vanquished! But as his hair slowly grew back, Samson felt his strength return. He told no one, waiting for the time when he would need to use it. That moment came when the Philistines gathered together in the temple of their god to celebrate a feast day.

At one point someone had the

Judges 13–16

idea of bringing Samson in so that they could mock him. The poor blind man was led by the hand into the great hall by a boy and was made to stand in the middle, where everyone could see him. He was standing between the two columns that held up the building. When Samson realized where he was, he prayed to the Lord, "Remember me, Lord! Give me strength one more time!" Then he spread his arms and pushed against the columns with all his might. The columns creaked and then crumbled, and the entire building collapsed, crushing all who had crowded into it.

David and Goliath

Many years passed, and the Philistines continued to be dangerous enemies of the people of Israel. After some time the twelve tribes decided to come together and elect a king so that united they might stand stronger against their enemies.

Saul was the first king, and he led the army of Israel against the forces of the Philistines. The two armies were lined up on two hills, facing each other across a valley. One day a giant Philistine, heavily armed, appeared in the valley to challenge the Israelites. His name was Goliath.

"Let us avoid a full battle," he said. "One of you, come and fight me. If I win, you Israelites will submit to us Philistines. If your champion wins, we will submit to you."

Every day Goliath came out to repeat his challenge, and every day the Israelites became more afraid because they thought no one could defeat such a powerful warrior.

But God had not forgotten His people. One day a young shepherd boy called David came to the Israelites' encampment to visit his brothers. When he heard the challenge and saw the fear among the Israelites, David went to Saul and said, "I will fight this stranger."

"Impossible," answered the king. "You are just a boy; you will not even be able to wear any

armor!" "I don't need any," David replied. "When lions or bears attack the sheep, I attack and kill them. I will do the same with this Philistine. The Lord who has saved me from wild animals will also save me from him."

1 Samuel 17

With a slingshot in his hand and five smooth stones from the river in his pouch, David walked toward the giant, who started to laugh at him. But David said to him, "You come to me with a sword, a lance, and a javelin. I come to you in the name of the Lord my God, who will make you fall by my hands!"

Goliath moved toward David. The boy quickly took a stone from his bag and, with the sling-shot, hurled it against the giant. He hit him right in the middle of the forehead. Goliath fainted and fell to the earth. With one leap David was on top of him and, taking Goliath's sword, cut off his head. Seeing this, the Philistine army turned and ran while the soldiers of Israel chased after them.

David Becomes King

David, a young shepherd with no experience of war, had defeated the giant warrior of the enemy because God had been with him. And God also chose him to be king of His people.

There was among the people of Israel a wise man to whom the Lord gave important tasks. His name was Samuel. One day the Lord said to him, "Take that horn full of oil and go to Bethlehem, to Jesse's house, because among his children I have chosen a king who will one day succeed Saul."

Samuel left and, when he arrived at Jesse's house, asked to see all his sons. Jesse presented the first, and Samuel asked himself if this was the Lord's elected one. But the Lord answered him, saying, "Do not pay attention to his appearance; it is not he. People look at appearances, but I look in the heart."

Jesse then had all seven of his children pass in front of Samuel, and every time Samuel said that that one was not the one chosen by the Lord.

After the seventh, he asked, "Are these all your children?" Jesse answered, "There is one more, the smallest, who is in the countryside tending the flocks."

So Samuel said, "Send and fetch him here; I will not leave without seeing him."

The smallest was, in fact, David, a handsome youth with tawny-colored hair and beautiful eyes. When he stood in front of him, Samuel heard the voice of the Lord saying to him, "He is the one I have chosen." So Samuel took the horn full of oil and poured it on David's head, consecrating him as one special to the Lord.

Several years went by. King Saul died fighting the Philistines, and David took his place. David became a great king, who always tried to do what would please the Lord. When he did anything to displease Him, he was quick to ask the Lord's forgiveness.

The Lord was with him all the time, and David was able to defeat his enemies and enlarge his kingdom. He conquered the city of Jerusalem, making it the capital of his kingdom, and he moved the Ark of the Covenant there.

David was also a poet and a musician who, to honor the Lord, wrote many poems. These are called psalms, and they are a part of the Bible.

Solomon the Wise

After David, his son Solomon became king of Israel.

One night in a dream the Lord asked Solomon what gift he would like. "Give me wisdom," replied Solomon, "so that I will know right from wrong and how to govern my people well."

This request pleased the Lord, who said, "You did not ask me for a long life, or riches, or victory over your enemies, but for wisdom. Good. I will give it to you; I will make you wiser than any other. And I will also give you long life, wealth, and victory."

The wisdom of Solomon became famous. A scribe always stood near him to write down his decisions and teachings.

One time two women came to him. The first said, "We live in the same house and each of us gave birth to a child a few days apart. One night this woman's child died; she then replaced hers with mine. The child that she carries in her arms right now is mine!"

The second woman, however, protested, "No. The child is mine. It was yours who died!"

So Solomon had a sword brought and ordered a soldier to "cut the child in two and give a half to each of the two women!"

At these words the first woman said, "No, my lord, do not kill the child. I would rather

1 Kings 3; 10

it be given to the woman who is holding it!"

The second woman, on the other hand, said, "Very good, let it be divided. In this way it will be neither mine nor yours."

"Put the sword away," said the king to the soldier. "The baby will be given to the woman who wished it left alive. She is the real mother since she truly loved it."

Drawn by Solomon's fame, the Queen of Sheba came from her country in Arabia to visit the king, bringing in her caravan of camels many gifts of gold, precious gems, spices, and perfumes. When the Queen of Sheba had admired the wisdom of Solomon and all that he had built, she said, "Happy are they who are governed by you! Blessed is your God who made you king!"

The Temple of Jerusalem

From the time when it was built in the desert of the Sinai, the Ark of the Covenant had never had a permanent home. Solomon set about arranging the construction of a worthy site for this precious sign of the presence of the Lord.

He had Hiram, king of Tyre, send architects and precious cedar wood. Gold, silver, and gems were collected with which to decorate the building. Eighty thousand men cut the needed blocks of stone from a quarry, and another seventy thousand brought them to Jerusalem. Here, on the summit of Mount Zion, a great workshop managed to build the Temple of the Lord in just seven years.

The Temple of Jerusalem became famous the world over for its imposing presence and beauty. A great altar was erected in the open space in front of the Temple. Here the priests sacrificed animals and burned the first fruits and vegetables of the season brought by the people to be offered to the Lord. The main part of the building was made up of three rooms arranged in a row. The first was the atrium. The second, called the inner sanctuary, contained a gold candelabrum with seven arms and a table, on which rested twelve loaves of bread, the symbol of the twelve tribes which made up the people of Israel. The inner sanctuary also had a small altar made of gold, on which every morning and evening the priest for that day burned perfumed incense. The third and innermost room was called the most holy and was completely covered in gold.

When everything was ready, Solomon had the Ark of the Covenant carried to the most holy sanctuary in a solemn procession. Then, in the presence of all the people, standing before the altar, Solomon offered the Temple to the Lord, saying, "Lord, listen to us when we come to this place to pray!"

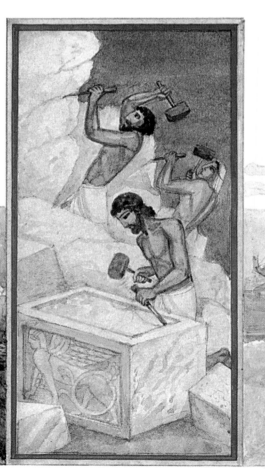

Elijah's Fire

*I*n spite of the advantages God gave His people, before too long they betrayed the Lord by worshiping the false gods of other peoples. So to remind them of their pact, the Lord sent them certain admonitions, or rather tasked a few men of great faith, the prophets, with speaking in His name.

One of the greatest of the prophets was Elijah. In his time almost all the Israelites worshiped a false god called Baal. To make everyone understand that Baal did not exist, Elijah

one day called the people and the priests of Baal together on Mount Carmel and made them this proposal.

"The priests of Baal will take a calf," he said, "and prepare it on their altar for sacrifice. I will do the same on the altar of the Lord with another calf. They will then call on Baal, and I will call on the Lord. Whichever answers by sending fire from heaven will be the true God."

All those present agreed to the challenge. For the whole morning the priests of Baal

called on their god, crying out and dancing around the altar. Elijah, looking on, encouraged them, "Shout louder! Maybe your god is sleeping or traveling!"

The morning passed and nothing happened. Elijah also erected an altar, placed wood on it and then the calf, and finally poured water over all of it. Then in a loud voice he prayed: "Lord, let it be known to all that You are the God of Israel and that I am Your servant."

He had not finished the prayer when a tongue of fire

1 Kings 18; 2 Kings 2

descended from the sky and, in a minute and in spite of the water, burned up the wood and the animal. Seeing this, the Israelites prostrated themselves with their faces to the ground exclaiming, "The Lord is God! The Lord is God!"

The fire sent by the Lord appeared again at the very end of Elijah's life. Elijah was walking beside his disciple Elisha, when he announced that he was about to leave him. Not long after, a fiery chariot drawn by flaming horses suddenly appeared and carried Elijah up into the sky. In this way Elijah left to take up the reward the Lord offers to His faithful friends.

Jonah: Three Days Inside a Whale

Jonah was another prophet chosen by the Lord. God said to him, "Go to the great city of Nineveh and warn those who live there that they must stop behaving so badly!" But Nineveh was a foreign city, and Jonah was afraid that its inhabitants would harm him. So he disobeyed the Lord and fled in the opposite direction. When he reached the sea, he embarked on a ship that would take him farther away. He went below the deck and fell asleep.

Very quickly a great storm came up on the sea and tossed the ship around until it threatened to break apart. To lighten it, the sailors threw all the cargo overboard. Then they called on their own gods, but this was in vain, for the storm got worse and worse. It occurred to them then that the storm might be caused by a god who was angry with one of the people on the ship. To find out who it might be, they cast lots and the lot fell to Jonah.

The sailors asked him, "Who are you? What wrong have you committed to bring down this punishment on us?" Jonah answered, "I am a Jew, and I fear the Lord God in heaven who made the sea and the land. Right now I am running from Him because I disobeyed His command. Throw me into the sea, and the storm will abate."

They did this, and that is what happened. But the Lord did not want Jonah to die. Instead, He sent a whale to swallow up and save Jonah, who stayed three nights and three days in the belly of the whale repenting of his disobedience. The whale vomited him up on the beach, on dry land.

Jonah then departed bravely for Nineveh, where he proclaimed what the Lord had instructed him to say.

The inhabitants of the city repented of their sins, begged forgiveness of God, promised to change their ways, and were saved.

The Fall of Jerusalem; Three Youths in the Furnace

Despite the warnings of the prophets, the people of Israel continued to commit acts that were wrong in the eyes of the Lord. Then a disaster befell them which was greater than any that had come before.

From the east came the powerful army of the Babylonians. They invaded the land of Israel, conquered Jerusalem, and destroyed it. Even the Temple that Solomon had built was razed to the ground and its treasures stolen. Many Israelites were taken prisoner and led off to live in Babylon.

The life of the Israelites, far from home and in a strange land, was hard. They began to reflect, and all of them came to understand the evil they had done in abandoning the Lord. But the Lord loved His people, and when He saw that they were repentant, He began to prepare for their liberation.

The Lord sent His prophets to console His people and to promise them that they would

return home. A few Israelites then helped others by setting a good example.

Here is what happened to three youths, Shadrach, Meshach, and Abednego. Nebuchadnezzar, the king of Babylon, had had a golden statue made and ordered that all should prostrate themselves before it and worship it. But the three young Israelites knew that they must worship only the Lord and decided not to obey the king's command. Brought before him, they said they were ready to endure his punishment rather than worship something that was not the Lord. The punishment was terrible: they were thrown into a fiery furnace.

But then there was a miracle. The king was amazed to see four

men walking in the middle of the fire; the fourth looked like the son of God. The three youths, instead of burning inside the furnace, passed through the flames all the while singing the Lord's praises. The king decided to free them, and because he recognized their miraculous deliverance, loyalty, and faith in God, Nebuchadnezzar asked them to work for him.

Return to Jerusalem; Waiting for the Messiah

Cyrus, king of the Persians, was the instrument the Lord chose to fulfill the prophets' promise that the people of Israel would return to their homeland. In the first year of his reign, Cyrus gave the Israelites permission to leave. Those who accepted the offer were mostly from the tribe of Judah, and since then Israelites have also been called Judaeans.

When they returned home, they found their houses destroyed, the walls of the city demolished, and the Temple in ruins. But they were not discouraged. With the little means and the scarce labor available to them, they set about rebuilding the Temple and, when it was ready, they dedicated it to the Lord.

Slowly life returned to normal, but quite differently from before. The Temple was not splendid as Solomon's once had been, and they no longer had their own king. Their land belonged to the king of Persia and after him to other powerful peoples nearby.

But the Israelites were sure that the Lord had not abandoned them. Their difficulties caused them to remember the times when their relations with

the Lord had been good and how serious had been their betrayal of Him. With the help of the prophets, they tried to follow God's law more faithfully while they also waited for more help from Him.

The prophets of the past had told of the arrival of an extraordinary messenger from the Lord, the Messiah.

The new prophets continued to speak of him and of what he would do.

Here is how the prophet Isaiah foretold his coming: "The people who were walking in the dark saw a great light. A child is born for us! On his shoulders he carries the emblems of the king. During his reign the wolf will live with the lamb, the leopard will lie down with the kid, the calf and the lion will feed together, and a child will lead them. The cow and the bear, together with their young, will go to pasture together. The lion will eat straw, without killing anymore; and babies will play without danger of snakes."

Among the people, the feeling of expectation was intense, and the hope placed in the new liberator was strong. And when the moment came, the long-awaited Messiah arrived.

NEW TESTAMENT

Our Father who art in heaven, hallowed be Thy name.
Thy kingdom come, Thy will be done,
on earth as it is in heaven.
Give us this day our daily bread,
and forgive us our trespasses
as we forgive those who trespass against us.
And lead us not into temptation, but deliver us from evil.
For thine is the kingdom, and the power,
and the glory, forever. Amen.

Matthew 6:9–13

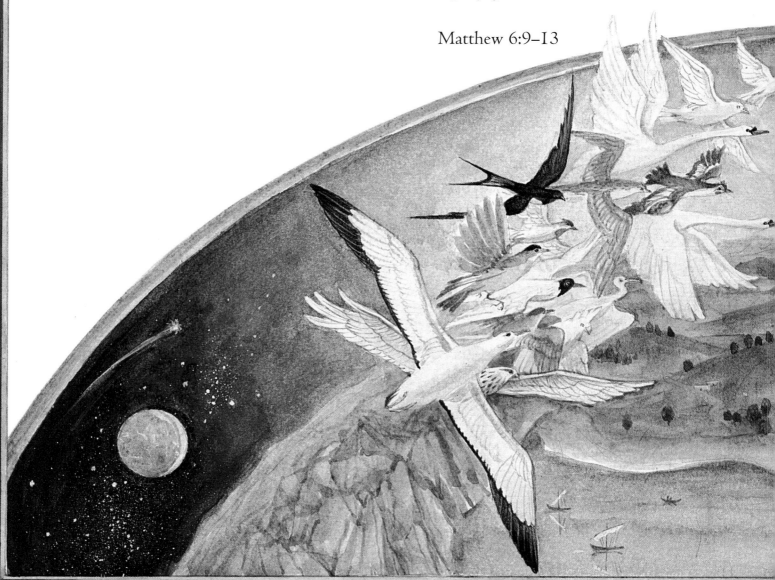

The Annunciation: "You Will Call Him Jesus"

The Annunciation: "You Will Call Him Jesus"

A young woman named Mary lived in the village of Nazareth in the land of Israel. When the Lord decided the time had come to send the Messiah foretold by the prophets, He sent the angel Gabriel to Mary. He appeared to her and greeted her, saying, "Rejoice, Mary, O favored one! The Lord is with you. The Holy Spirit will come upon you, and you will be the mother of a child whom you will call Jesus. Jesus, the Son of God, will be great, and his kingdom will have no end."

Mary answered, "I am the servant of the Lord; I am ready to do His bidding." The angel left her to find Joseph, the young man whom Mary was going to marry. He was a simple carpenter but a descendant of the great king David. The angel told Joseph that Mary was going to have a child, the Son of God.

At the same time, but in a different village, another child was expected with surprise and joy. His parents, Zechariah and Elizabeth, were very elderly. All their lives they had asked the Lord for a child, and now the Lord was to grant them one. Indeed, this child of theirs had a special task: he was to prepare the people of Israel to receive Jesus, the Messiah.

Zechariah and Elizabeth were relatives of Mary. When she learned from the angel Gabriel that Elizabeth was also going to have a child, Mary went to visit her. When she saw her approach, Elizabeth welcomed her with joy, saying, "Blessed are you among women, and blessed is your Son! You are blessed, because you believed in the Lord."

Mary stayed with Elizabeth for three months. Elizabeth gave birth to a son and he was named John.

The Birth of Jesus

At that time, the land of Israel was part of the Roman Empire. The emperor of Rome wanted to know how many men and women lived in his domain and ordered that a census be taken. This meant that every head of household had to register his family in the city of his forefathers.

Joseph was a descendant of David, and, therefore, he had to go to Bethlehem, which was the city of David. He had with him Mary, whom he had taken as his wife and brought to his home. When they arrived in Bethlehem, they found the city full of people who had come to be counted in the census. There was no more room for them at the inn, and they had to stay in a stable. That is where Jesus, the son of Mary and the Son of God, was born. Mary wrapped him in swaddling clothes and laid him in a manger.

In the nearby fields some shepherds were standing watch over their flocks. Suddenly they were surrounded by a great light, and an angel of the Lord said to them, "I bring you news of

Luke 2; Matthew 2

great joy, for in Bethlehem our Savior, Christ the Lord, is born!"

The word *Christ* has the same meaning as *Messiah.* The angel invited the shepherds to go and see the child. Suddenly the angel who had spoken was joined by many others, who sang, "Glory to God in the highest, and on earth peace to all those whom He loves."

The first people, then, whom God called to pay homage to His Son were the poorest and most humble. Soon after, however, very important people also came. Wise men, called Magi, arrived in Bethlehem from the East; they came riding camels, and they wore splendid clothing and brought with them a large train of servants. Studying the

sky, they had seen a new star, which they followed to Bethlehem. There they found Jesus, whom they recognized as the king of the Judaeans. These wise men knelt in front of the child and offered him their gifts: gold, a gift fit for a king; incense, which is a rare perfume; and myrrh, a precious ointment. They then returned to their homeland.

The Child Jesus Speaks in the Temple

Mary and Joseph returned to Nazareth, their village, with the baby Jesus. Jesus grew into a child who was good and always obedient to his mother, Mary, and to Joseph, whom all believed was his father.

But Jesus knew his real father was God, and one day he proved it.

As good Judaeans, Mary and Joseph went every year to Jerusalem for the great feast of Passover. When Jesus was twelve years old, they took him with them. As was the tradition then, they joined one of the many groups of pilgrims going to the holy city and traveled with them.

After the feast day had been celebrated, they began the trip home, still traveling in a group, and it was only at the end of the first day on the road that they realized that Jesus was not with them. They had all thought he was with relatives or friends, but in fact no one had seen him. They were worried, and so they went back and looked for him throughout the city.

Finally, after three days, they found him. He was in the temple, seated in the middle of the teachers, experts on the meaning of the Bible and all things concerning God. Jesus was listening to them, asking them questions, and speaking with them as an equal. The teachers were amazed at this youth who was so intelligent and knowledgeable.

Seeing him, Mary and Joseph let out a sigh of relief and marveled at the scene before them. Mary said to Jesus, "Son, why have you done this to us? We have looked for you anxiously!"

To these words Jesus answered, "Why were you looking for me? Did you not know that I must attend to the work of my Father, who is in heaven?"

. Jesus returned to Nazareth with his mother and Joseph. He continued to grow in both age and wisdom, and he was always obedient to Mary and Joseph.

Jesus Is Baptized

Jesus was about thirty years old when he decided to show the people who he really was and to begin to explain the reason for which he, the Son of God, had come into this world. He left Nazareth and went to the river Jordan.

He knew that there, for some time, many people had been coming to listen to his kinsman, John, the son of Zechariah and Elizabeth.

God had assigned John the mission of preparing the Jews for the coming of the Messiah promised by the prophets. To accomplish this he preached, encouraging everyone to repent of his or her sins and to be baptized as a sign that from that moment forward they were committing themselves to live according to God's wishes.

Because he baptized people, he was called John the Baptist, that is to say, John the Baptizer.

He warned, however, "I baptize you with water; but he who is coming after me is mightier than I. He whose sandals I am not worthy to carry will baptize you with the Holy Spirit!"

When John saw Jesus arrive, he announced to all those present, "Here is the Lamb of God, here is the one who will take away the sins of the world!" With these words John explained the reason for which

NEW TESTAMENT

Mark 1; John 1

the Son of God became man.

Jesus stood in line to have himself baptized. But John said to him, "You have no need; I instead should be baptized by you!" But Jesus said to him, "This is the way it should be!" So John baptized him.

The Holy Spirit then alighted on Jesus in the form of a dove, and at the same time a voice from heaven said, "This is my beloved Son; listen to him!"

Jesus Is Tempted

By receiving baptism from John in front of everyone, Jesus was recognized as the Son of God, and he was now ready to start his ministry. Because he was still a human being, however, Jesus also wanted to prepare himself for his mission. He went away into the desert, where he stayed for forty days without eating, to pray and think. After a while he became hungry, and the devil tried to take advantage of this to make him do something he should not.

There were many stones in the desert. The devil said to Jesus, "If you are really the Son of God, command this stone to become bread." But Jesus answered him with a saying from the Bible, "People do not live by bread alone, but by every word that comes from the mouth of God."

The devil then tried another course. He showed Jesus all the kingdoms of the world with all their riches and said, "All of this will be yours if you worship me and do as I say." But Jesus answered him with another phrase from the Bible, saying: "Love the Lord your God, and Him only will you serve!"

Trying for the third time, the devil also used a saying from the Bible. He took Jesus to the pinnacle of the Temple and said to him, "Throw yourself from here. It is written in the Bible that the angels will protect you, so that you will not harm yourself." But Jesus said, "The Bible also says: do not tempt the Lord!"

And thus defeated, the devil left.

Peter and the Other Disciples

One of the first things Jesus did at the beginning of his ministry was to call several men to join him. He invited them to become his disciples, to listen to and learn what he said so that they could eventually be his helpers.

One day when he was walking along the shore of the Sea of Galilee, he saw two fishermen, Peter and his brother Andrew, busy with their work. He knew that in their hearts these two men loved God. So he called them and said, "Come with me, I will make you fishers of men." Peter and Andrew dropped their nets at once and followed Jesus.

He did the same with another two brothers, James and John, who were also fishermen. To everyone's astonishment, he also called a tax collector to follow him. This was surprising because men who did such work were considered hardened sinners, since they gathered taxes for the Romans. But Jesus chose Matthew, and he dropped his work and followed the Lord. Matthew later wrote one of the Gospels, the four books that tell the story of the life of Jesus. John, the brother of James, wrote another of the Gospels.

Jesus chose twelve men from the disciples who followed him and called them apostles. They are like the pillars of the Church, which is itself the family of those who believe in the Lord Jesus. The biggest responsibility, however, Jesus chose to give to Peter.

One day Jesus asked his disciples, "What are people saying about me?" They answered, "Some think you are Elijah or another of the ancient prophets who has come back to the world." "And you," Jesus asked them, "who do you think I am?" Peter answered, "You are the Christ, the Messiah, the Son of the living God!" And then Jesus said to Peter, "Blessed are you because by yourself you could not have understood what you just said. My Father who is in heaven has revealed this to you. I say to you then, you are Peter and on this solid foundation I will build my Church, which nothing or no one will be able to destroy. I will give you the keys to the kingdom of heaven, and whatever you decide for the good of the Church I, in heaven, will approve."

The Wedding at Cana

*J*esus was invited to a wedding feast in Galilee, in the village of Cana. Mary, his mother, and the disciples were also invited.

In the middle of the celebration, the steward who had organized it found that the wine had run out. Without wine the feast would be ruined; but how could he get more?

This distressed Mary, and she said to Jesus, "They have no more wine." Jesus answered, "Truly, this is not something that concerns me." But Mary said to the servants, "Do whatever he tells you."

There were seven stone jars in the house, and each could hold about twenty-five gallons of water. Jesus said to the servants, "Fill the jars with water." Then, when they had filled them to the brim, Jesus said again, "Now take a bit of what is in the jars and carry it to the steward for him to taste."

The water had become wine, and the best quality wine! The steward said to the bridegroom, "Normally at a celebration the better wine is served first to the guests and then later, if it is needed, a wine of lesser quality.

You, on the other hand, have kept the best wine for the last!"

Changing the water into wine so that the wedding celebration would not be ruined was the first of many miracles which Jesus performed. Seeing what he had done, his disciples understood that he was the Christ, that is, the Messiah. They remembered the ancient prophets, who had said so many times that the Messiah would bring great joy to the people of God.

A Man Is Lowered through the Roof

*J*esus wanted what was best for everyone, and many of his miracles were to heal people who had a variety of problems. The lame, blind, leprous, and infirm gathered around him wherever he went, and he gave them back their health and happiness.

One day Jesus was in Capernaum, at Peter's house, where he was about to speak to a crowd of people. That day so many had come that there was not room for all of them in the house, and some had to stand outside in the street. Four more men joined them, carrying a paralyzed man on a stretcher. They wanted to bring him to Jesus so that he could make the man well again.

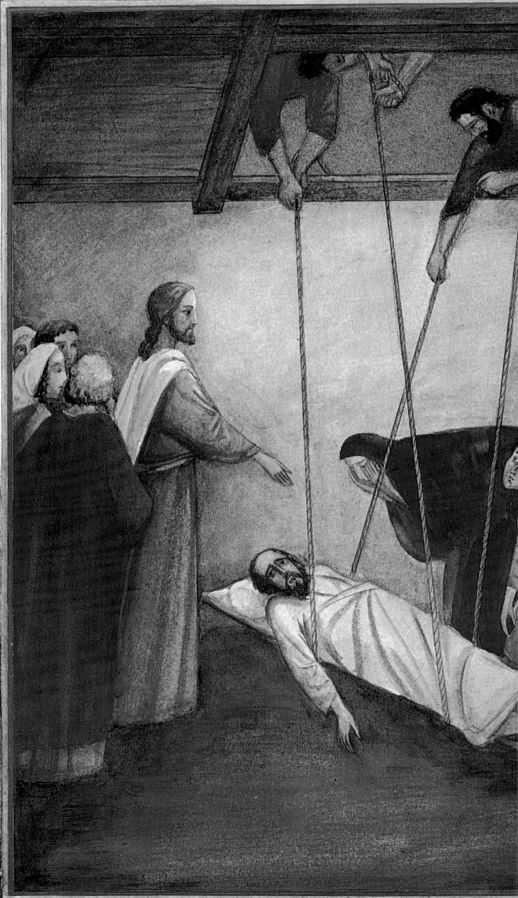

Since they could not get him into the house, they climbed up onto the roof, opened up the straw thatching, and lowered the stretcher down right in front of Jesus.

Seeing the faith of these men, Jesus intervened, but not in the way they had expected. He said to the paralyzed man, "My son, your sins are forgiven." By saying this, Jesus wanted everyone to understand a very important lesson, which is that the illnesses of the soul, its sins, are more serious than any sickness of the body.

But Jesus' words caused amazement among the people present, who thought, "What is this man saying? Only God can forgive sins!"

So Jesus, who can read thoughts, said, "Why do you think this? I will give you proof that I have the power to forgive sins. I will do something that you can see with your own eyes." Then, turning back to the paralyzed man, he instructed him, "Get up, pick up your stretcher, and return home!"

Immediately this man, who before had not even been able to move, sprang to his feet, completely cured, and he took his stretcher and went away. The people there were astounded and said, "We have never seen anything like this!"

The Sermon on the Mount

One day Jesus led his disciples up a mountain. Then he sat down and explained many important things to them. He told them which people would be blessed, that is, happy in an eternal life. He said:

"Blessed are the poor in spirit, because God will give them riches that no one will be able to take away.

"Blessed are those who suffer, because God will console them.

"Blessed are those who are not violent.

"Blessed are those who do what God wishes.

"Blessed are those who have compassion for others.

"Blessed are those who are pure in their hearts.

"Blessed are those who work to spread peace.

"Blessed are those who are persecuted because they have tried to carry out the will of God; God has prepared a great reward for them!"

He also said that these lessons completed the commandments God gave through Moses. And he reminded them that people see only the outer behavior of others. God, however, sees also into their hearts, and so it is not just our behavior but also our thoughts and feelings that should please God.

If someone is offended or wronged by another, that person must not seek revenge nor hate the one who committed the offense. In fact, he or she must pray for that person and help him in his need.

Jesus also taught that we must behave well, not to be admired by others, but to please God. For this reason it is better to do good without calling attention to it.

On another day Jesus spoke of the kingdom of heaven and described it in this way:

"The kingdom of God is like a treasure hidden in a field. When a person comes to know of it, he or she will sell everything in order to be able to buy the field."

"The kingdom of God is like a pearl merchant. One day the merchant finds the most beautiful pearl, one of great value, and so sells everything and buys that one pearl."

"The kingdom of God is like a net thrown into the sea that gathers fish of all types. When it is full, the fishermen pull it to the shore, sit down, and put the fish that are good to eat into crates to take to market whereas they throw away those that are not. That is what the end of the world will be like: the angels will separate the good people from the bad. The good will be carried up to the kingdom of heaven, and the bad will be thrown out."

The Bread of Life

One day Jesus and his disciples found themselves in a region along the Sea of Galilee where no one lived. Raising his eyes, Jesus saw a large crowd coming toward him, as often happened. He spoke in such a way and healed so many sick people that many came to be near him. Jesus spoke this time too, teaching the crowd many things about the kingdom of God, and he cured the infirm. No one, however, showed any sign of leaving for home. So Jesus said to Philip, "All these people must eat. How can we get food for them all?" And Philip observed, "The villages are far away, and anyway we do not have the money it would take to give them even a piece of bread each."

The apostle Andrew, Peter's brother, noted that one young man had five loaves of bread and two fish. He mentioned this to Jesus, saying, "It is not very much for all these people," because there were about five thousand of them. But Jesus ordered the disciples to seat everyone and to begin to distribute the bread and fish. When no one wanted any more, he had the remains gathered up. There were twelve baskets full of bread!

Seeing this great miracle, the crowd became very excited, and many said, "You must be our king!"

But that was not Jesus' inten-

tion. He withdrew, instead, to pray to his Father in heaven. The crowd returned home but came looking for him again the next day.

They found him in Capernaum teaching in the synagogue. He said to them, "You are looking for me because you hope that I will repeat the miracle of the loaves of bread. But listen to me instead. Those loaves of bread will satisfy your hunger for a few hours, but I will give you bread that will last for eternity."

Hearing these words, the crowd asked him, "Lord, give us some of that bread." And Jesus said, "I am the bread of life. Those who believe in me will not feel hunger or thirst again. I came down from heaven so that each person who believes in me will have eternal life." A few marveled at his speaking of having descended from heaven. But Jesus continued, "I am the bread of life, the living bread descended from heaven. Those who eat my flesh and drink my blood will have eternal life. Those who eat my flesh and drink my blood live in me, and I in them. Those who eat this bread will live forever."

Many did not understand Jesus' words, and even the apostles saw only later, when they had shared in the Last Supper with him, what he had meant.

Jesus Calms the Storm; Jesus Walks on Water

From time to time Jesus and his disciples took a boat to cross to the other side of the Sea of Galilee. On one of these trips, Jesus stretched out on the bottom of the boat and went to sleep. It was evening, and the sky was serene. All of a sudden a great storm came up, and the sea became very rough. The waves were higher than the boat, and the apostles were afraid. When water started coming in the boat, they were afraid it would sink. So they woke up Jesus, saying, "Lord, save us! We will all drown!".

Jesus said to the wind, "Be quiet!" and to the water, "Be still!" Without warning, the storm ended. Jesus said to the apostles, "Why are you so afraid? Do you not believe in me?" The disciples looked at one another and said, "What sort of man is this, our teacher, whom even the winds and water obey?"

Another time the disciples went in a boat without Jesus. The wind came up, and the waves began to rock the boat back and

Mark 4; Matthew 14

forth. Meanwhile, evening fell. The disciples rowed wearily, trying to get to the other shore in a hurry, but it was still far away.

Standing on the shore, Jesus saw that his disciples were in danger and wanted to help them. So he went toward them, walking on the water. When they saw a person walking on the waves, the disciples were terrified.

"Take heart, it is I! Do not be afraid!" said Jesus.

"Lord, if it is you, call me to come to you on the water!" Peter said to him.

"Come!" Jesus told him.

Peter began to walk on the water but very quickly he was overcome with fear and began to sink. He cried out, "Lord, save me!"

Jesus went to him, took his hand, and pulled him up, saying, "Why do you not trust me?" Then Jesus climbed into the boat along with Peter. Seeing this, the other disciples got down on their knees and exclaimed, "Truly you are the Son of God!"

The Transfiguration of Jesus

One day Jesus and his twelve apostles arrived at a village at the foot of a mountain. Leaving the others in the village, he took Peter, James, and John with him and climbed the mountain. When they reached the top, the three apostles witnessed a surprising and marvelous scene. Jesus was transfigured in front of them, that is to say, his appearance changed. His face shone like the sun and his clothes became white as snow. But this was not all! Moses and Elijah — the great commander who had led the people of Israel from Egypt to the promised land, and the most famous of the ancient prophets — appeared beside him.

With great excitement, Peter exclaimed, "How beautiful it is, Lord, to be here! If you wish, I will make three tents, one for you, one for Moses, and one for Elijah. That way we will stay here forever!"

They were still speaking when a luminous cloud wrapped around them. Then they heard a voice saying, "This is my beloved son. Listen to him!" Immediately

the three disciples prostrated themselves with their faces on the ground, full of fear at hearing the voice of God. But Jesus came up to them, touched them, and said, "Rise up. Do not be afraid." They opened their eyes, and no longer saw anyone except Jesus, looking as he usually did. As they went back down the mountain, he said to them, "Do not tell anyone about this vision until I am risen from the dead." It was only later that they understood that by this transfiguration Jesus had shown them his full glory before their time. For a moment they had been able to see him as the angels and saints in heaven do.

The Parable of the Prodigal Son

Jesus frequently used parables to teach his lessons. Parables are made-up tales, a bit like riddles, and it is the listeners who must uncover their meaning. One day Jesus told the parable of the prodigal son who was a spendthrift.

"A man had two sons. One day the youngest said to him, 'Father, give me my inheritance now. I want to use it as I see fit.' Although displeased, the father let him do as he wished. He gave him the money that was waiting for him, and the son went away. He journeyed to a faraway place, where he indulged in amusements of all kinds and soon squandered his money.

"In order to survive, the youth was reduced to tending swine, a miserable job which did not pay him enough even to keep him from being hungry. So he thought, 'In my father's house the servants eat their fill, while I die of hunger! I behaved badly toward God and toward my father. I will return home to beg his forgiveness and to ask him to consider me one of his servants.'

"And this the boy did. He was still some distance away when his father saw him approaching. He often stared down the road in the hope that his son would return. He ran to meet the boy, threw his arms around his neck, and kissed

him. The son said, 'Father, I have sinned against God and against you. I do not deserve to be called your son.' But the father had not stayed long enough to listen. He was so happy he ordered the servants, 'Quick, bring my son a robe, sandals, and a ring.... Prepare a beautiful feast, and let's have a celebration.... My son has returned! I was afraid I had lost him, and instead I have found him again!'

"The whole house was busy, and soon the celebrating began. The older son, however, when he returned home and learned the reason for the party, became angry. He did not think it right to forget the pain his brother had caused his father and all the money he had spent. To celebrate, after that, seemed a bit too much!

"But the father took his older son aside and explained to him, 'You see, my son, you have always stayed with me and everything that is mine is yours. But your brother has understood that he made a mistake and has repented, and it is for this that we rejoice.'"

The parable was finished. The listeners understood that Jesus had been speaking of God, who has more goodness than any other father. Even when people commit sins, He is always willing to forgive them if they repent!

The Parable of the Good Samaritan

"What must I do so that I will live forever in paradise?" One day Jesus heard this question asked of him, and he answered in this way: "You should know that. What does the Bible say?"

"I know," replied the man who had asked the question. "You must love God with all your strength, and your neighbor as much as yourself. I know this. But who is my neighbor?"

To answer that question, Jesus told another parable. "A man was going from Jerusalem to Jericho, along the road that crosses the desert. Suddenly robbers appeared, beat him with clubs, and left him half dead on the side of the road, taking with them everything he had.

"Soon after, a priest of the temple went by on the same road. He glanced at the wounded

man and went straight on. The same happened with a passing Levite, a priest's assistant. Then it was a Samaritan's turn. When the Samaritan saw this man – his enemy, for the Samaritans and the Judaeans were enemies – on the ground, he got off his donkey. Then, taking wine and oil from his bag, he cleaned and tended the poor man's wounds. He put him on his donkey and took him to the nearest inn, where he continued to help him.

"Later, when he had to leave, he called the innkeeper, gave him money, and said, 'Take care of him. If this is not enough money I will give you the rest when I return.'"

Having finished the story, Jesus asked the man who had put the question to him, "In your opinion, of the men who went by on the road, who was the neighbor of the man attacked by the robbers?"

"He who had pity on him," came the answer. And Jesus concluded, "Right. You should behave like him!"

Loving your neighbor, then, means recognizing those who need us and giving them help.

The Parable of the Rich Man and the Poor Man

Jesus also told this parable about loving your neighbor.

"There was a rich man who lived with every comfort. He wore luxurious clothes, and every day he invited his friends to his house for delicious meals, which they all enjoyed. He did not, however, take care of poor Laza-rus, a beggar dressed in rags who came to his front door every day hoping for the rich man's scraps.

"The years went by like this until the poor man died. But all his sufferings were rewarded because angels came to take his soul up to heaven, and they placed him near the patriarch Abraham.

"On the other hand, when the rich man died, his soul was sent to hell, where it was tormented. From there he could see Abraham high up above him, and beside Abraham was the poor man Laz-arus, happy at last. 'I know him,' he thought. 'He will have com-passion for me.' So he cried out,

'Abraham, Abraham, you are the father of our people. Have pity on me. Here I am devoured by thirst. Send Lazarus to dip the end of his finger in water so that I can bathe my tongue in a drop of water!'

"But Abraham answered him, 'Son, remember that in your life you were very happy with your riches, while Lazarus received only ills. Now it is fair that he be comforted and you not. Besides that, between us there is a great chasm that cannot be crossed.'

"The rich man understood the bad things he had done but also understood that it was now too late. He remembered then that he had five brothers who were still living and who behaved as he had, and said, 'Father Abraham, at least send Lazarus to warn my brothers so that they too do not end up here in this place of torment.'

"In response to this request, Abraham reminded him, 'Your brothers have the Word of God, the Bible. They must pay heed to that!' 'If one of the dead goes to them they will change their lives,' tried the rich man again. But Abraham concluded, 'No. If they do not practice the Word of God, they will not be convinced even by someone risen from the dead.' "

The Parable of the Wise Maidens

To explain what the kingdom of God would be like, Jesus told this parable. "The kingdom of heaven is like ten maidens who were called to attend a bridegroom. They took their oil lamps with them and started off to meet the groom. But five of them were a bit foolish and forgot to take extra oil with them. Five others, however, were wise and brought a flask of oil as well as the lamp.

"The bridegroom was delayed, and when the maidens finished making themselves ready, they fell asleep. At midnight they awoke to a shout, 'Here is the bridegroom! Come out to meet him!'

"The ten maidens got up and found their lamps burned out. But the wise ones lit them again immediately with the extra oil they had brought, while the others did not know what to do. The foolish maidens asked the wise ones, 'Give us a bit of your

oil, because our lamps have burned out.' But the wise maidens replied, 'We cannot give you any or the oil may not be enough for us! Go instead into the city and buy some more oil.'

"While the foolish maidens were away at the shops buying more oil, the bridegroom arrived. The five wise maidens who were waiting with their lamps lit accompanied him to the wedding celebration, and the door was closed behind them! When the other maidens returned, they knocked on the door and said, 'Lord, Lord, open the door for us!' But the groom answered, 'I do not know who you are!'

"Always be ready, because you never know the day or the time when the Lord will call each of you."

WEEK 42

Zacchaeus in the Tree

When we read Matthew's story of Peter and the other disciples, we saw that in Jesus' time the men who collected taxes for the Romans were not popular with the Jews, who considered them traitors. The chief of the tax gatherers of Jericho was called Zacchaeus. Everyone detested him and stayed as far away from him as possible, and he in turn did not mix with the people. But when he heard that Jesus, the man so many were talking about, was on his way to the city, Zacchaeus was curious to see him.

So he went to meet the Teacher, who was walking slowly through the crowd. But Zacchaeus was short and could not see Jesus; so he decided to climb up a tree, the branches of which stretched out over the road where Jesus would be passing by.

When Jesus, still surrounded by the crowd, passed under the tree, he looked up and said, "Zacchaeus, come down quickly from there because today I am coming to your house."

Zacchaeus was stunned with amazement. How had Jesus known his name? And how was it that he wanted to go to the house of a tax collector, a "sinner"? Many of the people in the crowd were scandalized by Jesus' words, saying, "He is going to a sinner's house!"

Zacchaeus came down from the tree and started toward his

house. Slowly he felt a great joy growing in his heart. The honor of receiving Jesus made him think about his life up to that moment. He understood the wrongs he had done to so many people and the sins he had committed every time he had failed to practice the Word of God. He decided to change his life. When Jesus entered his house, Zacchaeus said to him, "Lord, I will give half of my wealth to the poor, and if I have taken more than was right from anyone, I will give them back four times that amount."

Jesus said to him, "Today you had the wisdom to accept the salvation that the Lord God offered you. I have come to find and save those who in moving away from God might have been lost."

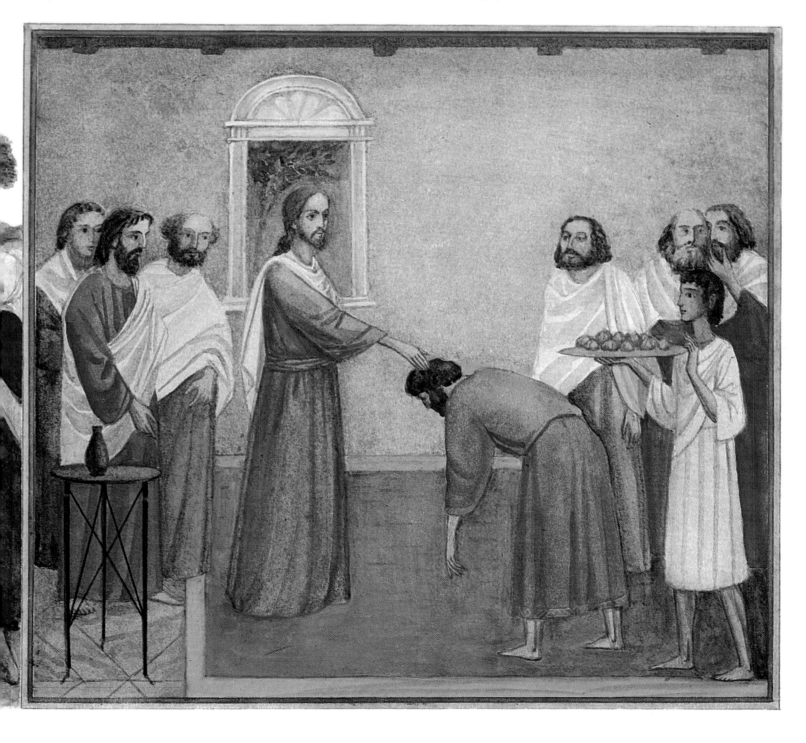

The Raising of Lazarus

*I*n the village of Bethany, not far from Jerusalem, a man lived with his two sisters; they were Lazarus, Martha, and Mary. They were friends of Jesus, who often came to see them and gladly spent time in their company.

One day while Jesus was far away, Lazarus became gravely ill. The sisters sent a message to alert Jesus so he would come quickly to cure his friend, as he had cured so many he did not even know. But Jesus did not hurry; in fact, he let several days go by on purpose. He had a plan and explained it to the apostles: "Lazarus is now dead. But I will wake him up."

When Jesus and the apostles reached Bethany, Lazarus was dead and had been buried four days before. Martha, in tears, said to him, "Lord, if you had been here, my brother would not be dead!" "Your brother will rise again," Jesus answered her. "Whoever believes in me, even if he or she is dead, will live for eternity. Do you believe this?" "Yes, Lord," said Martha, "I believe that you are the Christ, the Son of God!"

Meanwhile Mary also arrived,

accompanied by the many friends and relatives who had come to console her. Jesus asked them all to go with him to the tomb where Lazarus had been buried. It was a cave, sealed by a boulder. "Take away the stone," ordered Jesus. When the stone was rolled away, Jesus prayed to God the Father and called out in a loud voice, "Lazarus, Lazarus, come out!"

Then the unbelievable happened. The dead man came out of the tomb. He was still wrapped in the cloth used to bury the dead in those days, but he was walking around and talking. He had returned to life!

This astounding miracle convinced many people who came to believe in Jesus. Others, however, went to report him to the author-

ities, who were already concerned about his immense popularity among the common people. "Soon everyone will believe in him," the leaders of the people remarked to each other, "and they will no longer obey us. We must get rid of this Jesus." And they began to plot a way to put him to death.

Jesus' Triumphal Entry into Jerusalem

For three years Jesus had traveled around the land of Israel, moving from one city or village to another, to spread his good news. He told people the moment had come and that God was offering everyone the opportunity to be His friend. Jesus himself had made this possible, and now he was ready to die and be resurrected from the dead to fulfill his Father's mission.

The story of Jesus' sacrifice began a few days before Passover. As he did every year, Jesus traveled to Jerusalem with the apostles to celebrate the holiday there. Having arrived near the holy city, in the village of Bethphage, Jesus said to two of his apostles, "Go into the village. You will find there a donkey and its colt. Untie them and bring them here. If the owner asks you about it, tell him, 'The Lord needs them but will return them to you,' and he will let you take them."

And so they did this. The apostles then placed a cloak over the donkey's back, and Jesus climbed up on it and went on his way. While he was still outside the walls of Jerusalem, a large crowd welcomed him as if he were a king. The people spread their cloaks on the road and cut palm and olive branches and waved them as a sign of celebration. They called out greetings, saying, "Hosanna! Blessed is he who comes in the name of

the Lord! Long live the king of Israel!"

But this triumph worried the leaders of the people of Israel even more. "Look, everyone follows him," they said among themselves. "Acclaiming this man as a king is dangerous! The Romans, our bosses, could be offended because the only king is the emperor of Rome. We risk the emperor's sending his soldiers to destroy the temple and perhaps even killing us all."

They decided it was best to put Jesus to death and came to an agreement with one of the apostles, Judas Iscariot. In exchange for thirty silver pieces, Judas promised to lead them to a place where they could arrest Jesus without the crowd coming to his defense.

The Last Supper

As Moses had ordained it, the Jews celebrated Passover as a family meal. This ritual reminded everyone of God's great assistance to His people when they were enslaved in Egypt. The apostles were Jesus' family, and two days before the holiday, he gathered them together for the meal, the last of his earthly life.

In those times, the head of the household had his servants wash the feet of all the guests before they sat down at the table. That evening Jesus himself filled a basin with water and went around the table washing the feet of all the apostles. He explained, "If I, your Lord, have made this gesture of love to you, even more should you do the same for each other. Love one another as I have loved you. From this I will know that you are my disciples."

They began to eat, and then Jesus told them something that shocked them all. He said, "Truly, one of you will betray me." It is indeed true that God reads what is in people's hearts!

Unable to believe this, the apostles asked one another who this traitor could possibly be.

John 13; Matthew 26; 1 Corinthians 11

They asked the Teacher, and he answered, "It is he who dips his bread into my plate. It would have been better for him not to have been born!" "Teacher, is it I?" asked Judas, impudently. And Jesus answered him, "You have said so yourself." Seeing that he had been discovered, Judas left and went to finish what he had started.

A little later in this last, memorable supper, Jesus did something his disciples would never forget. He took a loaf of bread, blessed it, broke it, and distributed the pieces to all those present, saying, "Take this all of you and eat it, for this is my body that I offer in sacrifice for you." Then he took a cup of wine, blessed it, and passed it to the

apostles, saying, "Take this all of you and drink it, for this is my blood that must be shed so that all may receive forgiveness for their sins." Then he gave them a command, "Repeat this in memory of me."

The Passion: Jesus Prays, Is Betrayed, and Condemned

After supper, Jesus led his apostles to a garden of olive trees called Gethsemane. There he went off by himself for a while and prayed to the Father. Knowing what was about to happen he said, "Father, spare me this suffering. And yet, what will happen shall not be what I wish, but what you wish."

He returned to the apostles and found them asleep. He woke them up and said, "Now is the time when I will be given over into the hands of my enemies. He who has betrayed me is approaching." In fact, shortly thereafter a group of soldiers arrived, armed with swords and clubs. Judas was showing them the way and said to them, "The one you want is the man I will kiss."

Judas came up to Jesus and said, "Greetings, Master!" and kissed him.

The soldiers bound Jesus and

led him in front of the highest court of the land, where he was judged by the leaders of the people of Israel. These men lied in their accusations against Jesus, but in spite of it, they failed to prove any guilt on his part. Finally the head priest, Caiaphas, asked him, "Are you really the Christ, the Son of God?" and when Jesus answered yes, Caiaphas shouted, "He blasphemes! You have all heard what he said. We do not need any further testimony! What more do you need?" "He is guilty and deserves to die," answered the other leaders.

They did not, however, have the power to condemn him to death. According to the law, this could only be done by the Romans. So the leaders of the people sent Jesus to the Roman governor, Pontius Pilate, who alone could sentence a prisoner to die.

Pilate interrogated Jesus and found no guilt in him. He would have liked to free him, but the crowd, whose emotions had been whipped up by their leaders, shouted, "Death! Put him to death!"

Pilate made one last attempt. "For Passover it is traditional to pardon one prisoner. Do you wish me to free Barabbas, or this Jesus?" Barabbas was an assassin. But the crowd, spurred on by the leaders, cried, "Free Barabbas! Death to Jesus!"

The death penalty meant cruel torture that ended in crucifixion. Even Jesus suffered greatly. They whipped him, put a crown of thorns on his head, and placed a heavy cross on his back and made him carry it up a hill called Calvary. There they nailed him to the cross so that he would die slowly while suffering horribly.

Two thieves were also crucified, one on either side of Jesus.

The Passion: Jesus Dies and Is Buried

*A*ll of the apostles had run away because they were afraid of being killed along with Jesus. Only John accompanied Jesus all the way to Calvary and stayed at the foot of the cross with Mary, Jesus' mother. When he saw them, Jesus asked John to take care of Mary as if she were his mother too, and he asked Mary to consider John as her son.

A mob gathered at the foot of the cross, and the people mocked Jesus, saying, "He has saved others but cannot save himself! Come down from the cross. If you do, we will believe you."

They did not know that, had he wanted to, Jesus could have saved himself even before Judas' betrayal. But then the mission he had been sent to complete would not have been accomplished!

Jesus had compassion for the soldiers who had crucified him as well as for the crowd who scorned him. He raised his eyes to heaven and prayed, "Father, forgive them, for they know not what they do!"

Even one of the two men crucified beside him insulted him, but the second chastised the first. "What are you saying?

NEW TESTAMENT

John 19; Luke 23

We are condemned for our crimes; he, though, is innocent." And turning to Jesus he said, "Remember me when you are in your kingdom." And Jesus promised him, "Today you will be with me in paradise."

At about three o'clock in the afternoon, Jesus cried out, "Father, into Your hands I commend my spirit!," and then he died.

Shortly afterward a few friends took his body down from the cross and placed it in a tomb nearby. They sealed the tomb by rolling a big stone in front of it.

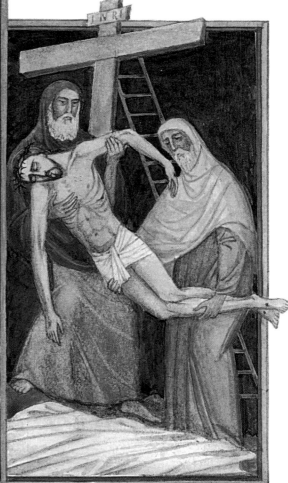

Jesus Has Risen! The Apparitions of Jesus

Jesus died and was buried the day before the Sabbath on which the Jews celebrated Passover. The day after the Sabbath, Mary Magdalene, a woman who was one of Jesus' friends, went to the tomb, and there she found the stone rolled away. She walked in and found Jesus' body gone!

When she recovered from her surprise, Mary hurried to Peter and John and said, "They have taken the Lord from the tomb, and we do not know where they have laid him!" The two apostles ran to verify this story and found that it was true. Then they remembered that Jesus had predicted, "The third day I will rise again."

Peter and John returned home. Mary, though, stayed near the tomb and wept. All of a sudden she heard a voice asking her, "Why are you crying?" Thinking that it was the caretaker, she said to him through her tears, "If you have taken the body, tell me where you have put it and I will get it!"

But the person who had spoken to her said, "Mary!" So Mary turned around, saw him, and recognized him. It was Jesus.

Jesus, then, was alive; he really was risen from the dead! The woman was beside herself with emotion and was made even happier when Jesus said to her, "Go tell others that you have seen me. Tell them also that I am going to

my Father and your Father, who is my God and your God."

Mary went and spread the news. That very evening, while the apostles were meeting together behind locked doors because they feared being arrested, they suddenly found that Jesus was with them. He showed them the wounds he had suffered during the crucifixion so they could be certain it was really he. And then he explained to them what their mission was from that moment on: "As the Father has sent me, so I send you out to be with the people. Those who forgive others their sins will themselves be forgiven in heaven, and those who will not forgive will not receive forgiveness."

On that same day, the day after the Sabbath, the risen Christ also appeared to two of his disciples who were walking toward the village of Emmaus. They did not recognize him, and he explained to them everything the prophets had foretold. He also told them that the Messiah had not come in order to restore the kingdom of Israel but instead to give all people the chance to enter the kingdom of God.

When they arrived in the village, the two disciples invited him in to eat with them. At the table Jesus took the loaf of bread and broke it as he had at the Last Supper. Finally they recognized him, but at that very moment he vanished from their sight.

Jesus Returns to His Father: The Ascension

After his resurrection from the dead, Jesus met many times with his apostles and other people.

Peter and his friends had returned to their work as fishermen. Once they exhausted themselves by working all night but did not catch anything. As dawn approached, while they were rowing back to shore, they saw a man on the beach urging them to cast their nets again. The apostles obeyed and pulled in so many fish that their nets came close to breaking.

Then they understood who this man was. They went toward the shore, and Peter threw himself into the water because he could get there faster by swimming. They found Jesus there; he had lit a fire, and beside it some loaves of bread were ready for them. "Bring

John 21; Acts 1

some fish," he said. "We will roast them and eat together."

During this time, Jesus entered houses whose doors were locked, heard what was being said in his absence, appeared and disappeared, and walked with his friends and encouraged them to believe in the Word of God.

Forty days went by like this, but then Jesus put an end to these encounters. He led his apostles up the Mount of Olives and spoke to them for the last time. He promised them the gift of the Holy Spirit, who is the third person of God after the Father and Jesus. With the help of the Holy Spirit they would be able to carry out the mission assigned to them. What mission? Jesus himself summed up their charge in this way, "Go throughout the world and invite everyone to become my disciple. Teach them what I have taught you and baptize them in the name of the Father, the Son, and the Holy Spirit. I am going to join my Father, but I will also be with you until the end of the world."

After saying this, Jesus rose up from the ground and continued to rise until a cloud took him out of their sight. Then two angels appeared and said to them, "Do not keep looking upward. Jesus has gone to his Father and your Father. He will come again at the end of time."

The Gift of the Holy Spirit: The Pentecost; Peter Baptizes

The feast of Pentecost fell ten days after Jesus' ascension into heaven. It was one of the great holidays of the year, and on that day all Jews gathered in Jerusalem, coming there from all the different places where they had settled. The city overflowed with foreigners. They were all Jews, but they seemed very different to each other because they spoke many languages and dressed like the people among whom they lived.

The apostles were joined in their house by Mary, the mother of Jesus, and by a group of disciples. Suddenly the Holy Spirit descended; the house shook with the sounds of a strong wind, and tongues of flame alighted on the heads of everyone there.

A miracle! Until that moment the apostles had been full of fear and in hiding, but now they felt strong, brave, and full of joy. They went outside and, finding a crowd that was curious about the reason for the noise, began to speak of Jesus and to invite the

people in the crowd to become his disciples.

Miracle of miracles, the listeners, who came from many places and spoke different languages, heard the apostles speaking in their own languages and were able to understand their preaching! Peter did most of the speaking and was so convincing that, when he finished, many asked him, "What then must we do?"

Peter answered, "Repent of your sins, have yourselves baptized in the name of Jesus, and you will receive the Holy Spirit." Many believed he was speaking the truth. That day about three thousand people had themselves baptized. By doing this they became part of the Church, the family of Jesus' disciples, Christians.

The Church began to grow. Everyone admired the Christians because they were good people and loved each other. Those who had wealth gave it to the apostles, who in turn distributed it to those who were in need. They gathered to pray together and, once a week, the first day after the Sabbath, they remembered the resurrection of Jesus. For this reason they named this day "the Lord's Day," which we call Sunday.

Peter and the Crippled Man; Peter and John; Stephen the First Martyr

One day Peter and John went to the temple to pray. At the door they met a cripple begging for alms. He stretched out his hand to the two apostles hoping for a coin, but instead Peter said to him, "I have no money but what I have I will give to you. In the name of Jesus Christ, rise up and walk!"

The cripple, healed, got up and began to leap for joy. He then went into the temple to thank God. Many people had seen the miracle. Peter said to them, "Pay no attention to us. It was not we who cured this man; it was instead the work of God and faith in Jesus."

They were in the midst of explaining who Jesus was when some soldiers, sent by the leaders of the people, came to arrest them. They did so and took the two apostles to prison. The leaders had thought that once Jesus was dead he would no longer be talked about. Instead, the number of people who called themselves Christians was growing!

The two apostles were brought in front of the court. The elders forbade them to speak any more of Jesus, but Peter answered, "Is it more right to obey you or God? We cannot be silent about what

we have seen and heard." They did not stop talking about Jesus, and they continued to heal the sick.

Unable to silence the disciples, the popular leaders began to persecute the Christians. Peter was thrown in jail, but the Lord sent an angel in the night to free him.

Stephen, a courageous and wise young man who worked with the apostles, was also arrested. He was accused of speaking against Moses and against God. The accusations were false, but during the trial the judges pretended to believe these charges in order to condemn Stephen. At one point Stephen told them, "Right now I can see the heavens opening, and Jesus is seated to the right of God." So the judges accused him of blasphemy and condemned him to die. He was dragged outside the city and stoned to death.

While he was being pelted by the stones, Stephen prayed, "Lord Jesus, receive my spirit." Then, remembering the words that Jesus had uttered on the cross, he also prayed for his killers, saying, "Lord, forgive them for their sins."

The Story of Paul; On the Road to Damascus; Escape from Damascus

Those who had stoned Stephen had given their cloaks for safekeeping to a young Jew named Saul. He became a great persecutor of Christians, taking men and women away from their homes and putting them in prison. The popular leaders sent Saul to Damascus to arrest the Christians in that city and gave him an escort of soldiers to take with him.

Saul was traveling along the road to Damascus when an extraordinary thing happened. A brilliant light shone from the sky and was so strong he could not bear to look at it. He closed his eyes and fell to the ground. A voice then said to him, "Saul, Saul, why do you persecute me?" "Who are you?" asked Saul, and he heard the voice answer him, "I am Jesus whom you are persecuting."

Saul was overwhelmed. "What must I do?" he asked, and Jesus explained, "Get up and enter the city. There you will be told what you are to do." Saul got up, opened his eyes, and realized that he had gone blind.

The soldiers accompanying Saul took him by the hand and led him to the city of Damascus.

There the Lord said to Ananias, a Christian who lived there, "Go to the street called Straight. You will find there a man named Saul. Place your hands on his eyes so that he may recover his sight." Ananias protested, "Lord, I have heard about this man. I know he has persecuted your faithful in Jerusalem and has come to Damascus to do the same." But Jesus replied to him, "Do as I have said. I have chosen this man to make my name known to all people."

Ananias went to Straight Street, found Saul, and said to him, "Saul, my brother, the Lord who spoke to you along the road has sent me to you." Ananias stretched out his hands, and Saul regained his sight. He was baptized immediately. From that moment on, he changed his life; he proclaimed Jesus and brought new disciples to the Church. As a sign of his new life, Saul changed his name to Paul.

Some of the Jews of Damascus could not bear his preaching, which they considered a betrayal, and they hatched a plot to kill him. But Paul learned of their plans. He had himself lowered down from the city walls in a basket and escaped.

The Story of Paul: His Travels, Miracles, and Letters

Obeying the will of the Lord, Paul traveled widely to tell people everywhere about Jesus. Paul undertook four long voyages, going by sea and by land, and traveling with a group of disciples. These journeys were as full of risks and dangers as they were of surprises and adventures, but they were also always fruitful.

In the city of Lystra, Paul healed a man who had been lame since birth. Seeing the miracle, the people exclaimed, "The gods have come among us in human form!" They thought that Paul was their god Hermes and his companion, Barnabas, their god Zeus. The people offered animal sacrifices to their divinities. The priest of Zeus went to the temple with a bull that he intended to sacrifice and was followed there by a crowd of people. But Paul and Barnabas intervened, saying, "Do not do it! We are humans, as you are! Indeed, we have come to urge you to abandon these false gods and to convert you to the true God!"

At Philippi, Paul was put in prison and shackled to the wall with iron chains. During the night an earthquake shook the prison; his chains came loose, and the doors were thrown open. Thinking that all the prisoners had escaped, the jailer decided to kill himself. But Paul cried out, "Do not do it, we are all still here!" So the jailer took Paul home, washed his wounds, and prepared food for him. Paul took advantage of this to talk to him about Jesus. The jailer believed what he said and was baptized.

Paul was often persecuted, beaten, hunted down, and put in jail. He almost died near the island of Malta when the ship on which he was traveling sank. But he never gave up. Wherever he went he proclaimed Jesus, and in many cities he founded new communities of Christians. When he left, he wrote them letters to teach them more about faith in God and to urge them to put their faith into practice.

The End of Time

One day when he was speaking to a crowd, Jesus told them, "At the end of time I will return, I will sit on a throne and call before me all people. I will divide them into two groups, the good and the bad, and I will say to the good, 'Come, you who are blessed by my Father, inherit the kingdom prepared for you. Because I was hungry and you gave me food, I was thirsty and you gave me drink, I was homeless and you invited me in, I was naked and you clothed me, I was sick and you cared for me.' The righteous will ask me, 'When, Lord, did we do this?' And I will answer, 'Every time you did that for one who needed it, you did it for me.'"

The kingdom being made ready for everyone who loved his or her neighbor is paradise. The Bible compares it with Jerusalem but in a way intended it to mean that it is much more beautiful than the holy city we can see on earth.

The heavenly Jerusalem shines with the glory of God. It is made of gold, pearls, and precious stones. It needs neither the light of the sun nor of the moon because it is illuminated by God's splendor. Those who live there will be happy. They will suffer no more pain, and there will be no death. All will praise God with songs and will live for centuries without end.

What a marvelous prospect it is, to live forever with Jesus! The first Christians longed for this to happen, and so they often repeated the prayer, *"Maranà tha,"* which means, "Our Lord, come!" Apocalypse, or Revelation, the last book of the Bible, tells of

NEW TESTAMENT

Matthew 25; Revelation 21–22

the heavenly Jerusalem and concludes with this prayer of the first Christians, "Come, Lord Jesus!"

Comparative Chronological Table

B.C. dates	Biblical Events	General History
2600–2200		Great pyramids are built in Egypt
2130–2015		Dynasty of Ur; Sumerian civilization flourishes
2000–1700		Palace of Knossos and other splendors of the civilization of Crete
1850	Time of the patriarchs Abraham, Isaac, Jacob, and Jacob's twelve sons begins	
1815		First Assyrian empire is founded
1793–1750		Hammurabi, king of Babylon, draws up the first code of laws
c. 1600	Joseph, son of Jacob, goes to Egypt, followed shortly thereafter by his father and brothers	
c. 1600–1240	People of Israel live in Egypt	
1580–1200		Mycenaean civilization flourishes
c. 1300–1200		Ramses II and then Merneptah are pharaohs of Egypt
c. 1240	Moses leads the people of Israel out of Egypt	
c. 1200	Twelve tribes of Israel conquer Canaan under Joshua's leadership	Philistines settle on the coast of Palestine
c. 1100		Phoenicians expand their power throughout the Mediterranean world. Splendors of the city-state of Tyre
c. 1030–1010	Reign of Saul; prophet Samuel is active at this time	
c. 1010–970	Reign of David	
c. 970–931	Reign of Solomon; construction of the first Temple in Jerusalem	
969–936		Hiram is king of Tyre
931	Division of the kingdom into the kingdom of the north, or the kingdom of Israel, and the kingdom of the south, or the kingdom of Judah	
931–722	Duration of the kingdom of Israel. Seventeen kings from different dynasties succeed one another. Prophets Elijah and Elisha are active	
931–586	Duration of the kingdom of Judah. Nineteen kings, all descendants of David, succeed one another. Prophets Josiah, Micah, Isaiah, Jeremiah, and Ezekiel are active during this time	

B.C. dates	Biblical Events	General History
896–612		Assyrians conquer Mesopotamia and extend their power in the Near East
814		Carthage is founded
776		First Olympiad is held in Greece
753		Rome is founded
722	Sargon II of Assyria destroys Samaria, capital of the kingdom of Israel	
721	People of the kingdom of Israel are deported to Assyria	
701	Sennacherib, king of Assyria, lays siege to Jerusalem	
626–539		Neo-Babylonian empire
587	Nebuchadnezzar, king of Babylon, lays siege to Jerusalem	
586	Babylonians conquer the kingdom of Judah, deport all inhabitants, and destroy Jerusalem and the Temple	
539		Cyrus II, king of Persia, conquers the Babylonian empire
538	Edict of Cyrus allows the Jews to return to their homeland	
522–486		Darius I is king of Persia
520–515	Reconstruction of the Temple in Jerusalem	
498–480		Greeks defeat the Persians at the battles of Marathon, Thermopylae, and Salamis
461–429		Golden Age of Pericles; Parthenon is built in Athens
336–323		Reign of Alexander the Great
332	Alexander the Great conquers Palestine	
323–280		Conflict among the Diadochi, successors to Alexander. In Egypt the Ptolemies come to power and in Syria the Seleucids
323–197	Ptolemies rule in Palestine	
197	Palestine is conquered by the Seleucids of Syria	
167–142	Maccabees rebel against Syrian persecution	
146		After centuries of struggle (the Punic Wars), Romans destroy Carthage

B.C. dates	Biblical Events	General History
63	Romans conquer Palestine	
44		Julius Caesar dies
40	With consent of the Romans, Herod the Great becomes king of Palestine	
30		Romans conquer Egypt
29		Augustus, first emperor of Rome, takes power

A.D. dates	Biblical Events	General History
4	Herod the Great dies; kingdom is divided among his sons Archelaus, Herod Antipas, and Philip	
6	Archelaus, king of Judaea, Samaria, and Idumaea, is deposed; kingdom is governed directly by Roman procurators	
6–7	Birth of Jesus	
14		Augustus dies; Tiberius succeeds him
26–36	Pontius Pilate is Roman governor of Judaea, Samaria, and Idumaea	
30	Crucifixion and resurrection of Jesus; Pentecost	
c. 36	Conversion of Paul	
37–41		Caligula is emperor of Rome
41–54		Claudius is emperor of Rome
c. 43	Paul begins his ministry	
54–68		Nero is emperor of Rome. Burning of Rome and the first persecutions of Christians
60	Paul in Rome for the first time	
64–67	Martyrdom of the apostles Peter and Paul	
66	Judaeans stage an armed rebellion against Romans	
69–79		Vespesian is emperor of Rome. Construction of the Coliseum begins
70	Romans destroy Jerusalem and the Temple	
c. 104	John, the last apostle, dies	
130	Hadrian rebuilds Jerusalem and calls it Aelia Capitolina	

For Harry N. Abrams, Inc.:
Project Coordinator: Ellen Cohen
Copy Editor: Joanne Greenspun
Design Coordinator: Dirk Luykx
Typographic Designer: Tina Thompson
For Happy Books:
Art Director: Dana Camerini

Library of Congress Cataloging-in-Publication Data
Brunelli, Roberto.
[Sacra Bibbia. English]
A family treasury of bible stories : one for each week of the
year / retold by Roberto Brunelli ; illustrations by Mikhail
Fiodorov ; translated from the Italian by Lawrence Jenkens.
p. cm.
Summary: Presents fifty-two stories that retell the contents of
the Old and New Testaments of the Douay version of the Bible.
ISBN 0–8109–1248–1 (hardcover)
1. Bible stories, English.   [1. Bible stories.]   I. Fiodorov,
Michael, ill.   II. Title.
BS555.2.B7813   1997
220.9'505—DC21   96–54800

Published in 1997 by Harry N. Abrams, Incorporated, New York
A Times Mirror Company

Printed and bound in Italy

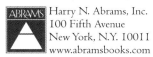 Harry N. Abrams, Inc.
100 Fifth Avenue
New York, N.Y. 10011
www.abramsbooks.com